THE K

THE KNOW OF THINGS

Derek O'Brien
in conversation with
**Jug Suraiya,
Bunny Suraiya
and Vikas Singh**

Illustrations by Neelabh Banerjee

PENGUIN BOOKS

Penguin Books India (P) Ltd., 11 Community Centre, Panchsheel Park, New Delhi 110 017, India
Penguin Books Ltd., 80 Strand, London WC2R 0RL, UK
Penguin Group Inc., 375 Hudson Street, New York, NY 10014, USA
Penguin Books Australia Ltd., 250 Camberwell Road, Camberwell, Victoria 3124, Australia
Penguin Books Canada Ltd., 10 Alcorn Avenue, Suite 300, Toronto, Ontario M4V 3B2, Canada
Penguin Books (NZ) Ltd., Cnr Rosedale & Airborne Roads, Albany, Auckland, New Zealand

10 9 8 7 6 5 4 3 2 1

Typeset in *Optima* by Mantra Virtual Services, New Delhi
Printed at International Print-O-Pac, Noida

Contents

Preface   vii

1. The Roots of Knowledge   1

2. The Great Knowledge Superbazaar   12

3. How Do We Know What We Know?   20

4. True and False Knowledge   28

5. Zen and the Art of Paradox Maintenance   38

6. The Never-ending Universe of Knowledge   48

7. The Third Wave and the Knowledge   60
   Worker

8. Managing Knowledge: Know Why and
   Know How   71

9. Info-clutter: When More Is Less   87

10. Who's Smart? Who's Not? Who Knows?   97

11. The Seamless Robe of KQ   106

Index   116

Preface

Knowledge is power.

For knowledge helps you to adapt to your environment better and so increase your chances of success. The more competitive and demanding the environment, the greater the need for knowledge.

When prehistoric humankind gained knowledge of fire and learnt how to sharpen sticks into spears, it vastly increased their chances of success—and survival—against other, seemingly more powerful, species.

In the last 100 years, we have acquired and put to use more knowledge than ever existed before in all of our recorded history.

In the new millennium, as we enter the knowledge era, what we know — and equally, what we don't know — is of even more crucial importance.

This is where KQ — or Knowledge Quotient — comes in. KQ is the first practical, demonstrable method of gauging and expanding your range of knowledge. Unlike the obsolete concept of IQ — or

Intelligence Quotient — KQ is not fixed and finite. KQ is like a stretchable elastic band which is capable of almost limitless expansion.

This book is not — nor does it even presume to be — a map of the realm of knowledge, nor even a sketchy outline of it. But it will have succeeded in what it set out to do if it acts as a signpost which indicates a few, a very few, of the myriad paths to the *terra cognita* of the known.

It is not a guide so much as an exploration. And that is why it is couched in the conversational style of an on-going discourse, rather than the authoritative mode of assertion.

But enough preamble. Derek, Jug, Bunny and Vikas are waiting to get on with it. Shall we join them?

CHAPTER 1

The Roots of Knowledge

Derek O' Brien: Lately, there's a lot of talk about the so-called knowledge industry. What's your take on this?

Jug Suraiya: Well, Derek, today, the knowledge industry is revolutionizing the world. Never before have so many people had such wide access to so much information and knowledge.

The knowledge industry is unique. The raw material of data it uses is as intangible as its final product. But every day it produces very tangible results worth billions of dollars. It is a smokeless industry, yet it sets our imagination afire like nothing else has ever done.

Knowledge transforms us and our universe. It is modern technology's answer to the Midas touch of mythology.

Derek: That's all very well and good. But when people talk about knowledge, do they know what they're talking about?

Jug: The funny thing about knowledge is that we have so little knowledge about it. What *is* knowledge? Human beings—who believe they are the only species which possess knowledge—have asked themselves this question for over 3,000 years.

What is knowledge? How do we know what we know? The study of knowledge and of the process of knowing is called epistemology. But the more answers that philosophers and thinkers try to supply regarding the definition of knowledge and its origins, the more questions they raise. Take the case of the ancient Greeks, Socrates, Aristotle and Plato.

Derek: Yes, let's have a look at what they said.

Jug: Socrates asked if knowledge comes from within us. And the Socratic method was largely an effort to draw out our innate knowledge about philosophical truths. But here's the man himself:

～

'And now,' I said, 'let me show in a figure how far our nature is enlightened or unenlightened: — Behold! human beings living in an underground den, which has a mouth open towards the light and reaching all along the den; here they have been from their childhood, and have their legs and necks chained so that they cannot move, and can only see before them, being prevented by the chains from turning round their heads. Above and behind them a fire is blazing at a distance, and between the fire and the prisoners there is a raised way; and you will see, if you look, a low wall built along the way, like the screen which marionette players have in front of them, over which they show the puppets.'

'I see.'

'And do you see,' I said, 'men passing along the wall carrying all sorts of vessels, and statues and figures of animals made of wood and stone and various materials, which appear over the wall? Some of them are talking, others silent.'

'You have shown me a strange image, and they are strange prisoners.'

'Like ourselves,' I replied, 'and they see only their own shadows, or the shadows of one another, which the fire throws on the opposite wall of the cave.'

'True,' he said, 'how could they see anything but the shadows if they were never allowed to move their heads?'

'And of the objects which are being carried in like manner they would only see the shadows?'

'Yes,' he said.

'And if they were able to converse with one another, would they not suppose that they were naming what was actually before them?'

'Very true.'

'And suppose further that the prison had an echo which came from the other side, would they not be sure to fancy when one of the passers-by spoke that the voice which they heard came from the passing shadow?'

'No question,' he replied.

'To them,' I said, 'the truth would be literally nothing but the shadows of the images.'

'That is certain.'

'And now look again, and see what will naturally follow if the prisoners are released and disabused of their error. At

first, when any of them is liberated and compelled suddenly to stand up and turn his neck round and walk and look towards the light, he will suffer sharp pains; the glare will distress him, and he will be unable to see the realities of which in his former state he had seen the shadows; and then conceive someone saying to him, that what he saw before was an illusion, but that now, when he is approaching nearer to being and his eye is turned towards more real existence, he has a clearer vision, — what will be his reply? And you may further imagine that his instructor is pointing to the objects as they pass and requiring him to name them, — will he not be perplexed? Will he not fancy that the shadows which he formerly saw are truer than the objects which are now shown to him?'

'Far truer.'

'And if he is compelled to look straight at the light, will he not have a pain in his eyes which will make him turn away to take refuge in the objects of vision which he can see, and which he will conceive to be in reality clearer than the things which are now being shown to him?'

'True,' he said.

‿

Jug: Socrates's ideas were jotted down by someone we would today call a rookie reporter, namely Plato, who said knowledge originated in a transcendent world of pure ideas of which the physical world was only an imperfect manifestation.

Derek: What about Aristotle? How did he differ from them?

Jug: Aristotle and his followers had the counter-proposition that knowledge was largely a process of acquiring and assimilating a series of experiences through our physical senses. But let's get it straight from the horse's mouth:

Everything which comes into being is brought about by something, that is, by a source from which its generation comes. And it is composed of something. Now this latter is best described not as the absence of the thing but as the matter from which it comes. And it becomes a particular thing, as a sphere or a circle or some other thing. Now one does not 'make' the material — as the bronze — of which a thing is composed; so one does not make the sphere, except in a secondary sense, in so far as the bronze circle is a circle and one makes it. For the act of making a particular thing is a process of making it out of some material in general. I mean that to make the bronze round is not to make the 'round' or the 'sphere', but quite a different thing — that of putting this form into what did not have it previously. If one made the 'form', one would make it out of something else, for this would underlie it, as when one makes a sphere out of bronze. This is done by making of a particular kind of substance, namely bronze, a special sort of thing, namely a sphere. And if one makes this 'sphere' also in the same way, it is evident that he will make it in the same manner, and the process of origination will go on to infinity. It is evident therefore that the form, or whatever one ought to call the shape of the perceived object is not 'made'. It does not 'become', nor does it have an origin. Nor is there any scope for the essential conception of a thing. For this is what is implanted in another entity, either by training or by nature or by force. But one does cause the 'bronze sphere' to be. For one makes it out of bronze and the form of 'sphere'. One puts the form into this matter, and it is then a bronze sphere. But if there is an origin for 'the idea of sphere in general' it will be something generated from something else. That which is generated will have to be analysed again in turn, and each reduced to something further, then that to something else; I mean in one aspect into matter, in another into form. A sphere is a figure whose surface is everywhere equally distant from a centre. One aspect of it is the material into which the form is to be put; the other the form which is to be put into it. The whole is what results, namely, the bronze sphere.

~

Derek: OK, so who won that argument? Aristotle and his lot? Or Plato, Socrates and their bunch?

Jug: Neither. After 3,000 years of debate, these and other arguments about knowledge still continue. And will do so as we acquire more and more knowledge about knowledge. And the more we know about knowledge, the less we really know about it. Or as Socrates once remarked: I alone of my contemporaries know something, because I alone know that I know nothing.

Is ignorance the true measure of Socratic wisdom? In other words, does it mean that the more knowledge we possess, the more questions we will ask ourselves about what we know?

Any answer we make, whether yes or no, will inevitably raise a further question.

If we answer 'yes', the question that comes up is how do we know that. And if we answer 'no', the question remains as to how we know *that*.

Derek: Whew! All this abstract stuff is great, but how do I put it to use in practical life?

Jug: Well asked, Derek. Though we do not, and perhaps never can, have a final, or philosophic, answer or end to knowledge, we certainly do, and indeed we must, have a working hypothesis of knowledge. For in the world of practical reality, knowledge works. It is useful to us in our everyday lives. In fact, without knowledge we would not have everyday lives. Perhaps to begin with we ought to distinguish between information and knowledge.

A fact such as the one that Mount Everest is the highest mountain in the world; or that Washington DC is the capital of the USA; or that India's first prime minister was Jawaharlal Nehru, constitutes information.

The ability to calculate the height of Everest; or to look up an atlas to locate Washington DC; or to write an essay on Nehru's role on the making of modern

India, involves knowledge.

Information is about the *what* of things. Knowledge is about the *how*. We should also distinguish between knowledge and intelligence. Intelligence is the capacity to connect; knowledge is *how* we connect, and to what purpose. Intelligence is the fire; knowledge is the heat of the fire which we can use to cook a meal, drive a steam turbine or send a rocket into space.

Knowledge, or the lack thereof, determines how well or badly we function in any given environment.

If, for example, a bushman of the Kalahari desert were suddenly to find himself in Manhattan he would not have the knowledge of how to cross a street at traffic lights, take a subway, withdraw money from a bank or avoid getting mugged. As a result, his chances of survival would be extremely slim.

On the other hand, a Manhattan executive making a million dollars a year would equally soon perish in the bushman's desert as he would not know where and how to find water, the roots of which plants to eat, and how not to get stung by a scorpion.

This does not mean that either the bushman or the executive is unintelligent, merely that they lack knowledge of their new environments. With training, the executive could well end up as the head of the desert tribe, and the bushman become the mayor of

New York City. The ability to acquire new forms of knowledge is not restricted by race, gender or social status.

Knowledge, literally, is freedom.

CHAPTER 2

The Great Knowledge Superbazaar

Derek: OK, Jug, we'd got to the bit where you'd said that knowledge is freedom.

Jug: That's right, Derek. Knowledge *is* freedom, and that includes freedom of choice.

Think of the realm of knowledge as a huge supermarket, a great bazaar, crammed with products of different brands for different uses. When you walk into the supermarket of knowledge you are confronted with a bewildering variety of competing products. What should you 'buy', and what should you leave out, at least for the time being? For obvious reasons you cannot buy the entire supermarket in one go. How would you carry it with you, and where would you store it?

Derek: What I do when I go shopping is carry a list with me.

Jug: Bang on, Derek. That's exactly it. When most of us enter the supermarket of knowledge we take with us — as we do when we go to a 'real' supermarket — a mental 'shopping list' of what we need for our day to day living, plus perhaps a few luxuries or delicacies — the knowledge equivalent of French perfumes or Swiss chocolates—with which we would like to indulge ourselves, even though they might not be necessary to ensure our immediate survival.

Take the case of Sherlock Holmes. The formidably erudite detective astounded Watson by admitting that he had not known, until Watson mentioned it, that the earth goes around the sun. When Watson expressed amazement at his friend's ignorance of a simple fact known by every schoolchild, Holmes testily retorted that this piece of knowledge was of no concern at all to him in his career as a detective and that, since Watson had gratuitously burdened him with it, Holmes would expunge it from his mind as soon as possible. The great detective — who among many other things had the knowledge of how to identify 140 different types of tobacco from the ash alone and who played a Stradivarius violin with virtuosity — likened the human brain to an attic which over the years became full of junk. So that unless you were very careful about what you put into your mental attic, pretty soon it would get so cluttered with useless lumber that you would not be able to find what you needed.

Derek: Well, when he puts it that way, it seems to make sense.

Jug: Yes, but Holmes's view of the human brain and its capacity to contain knowledge may seem out of date today, when science and technology have enabled us, through computers and other devices, to build 'outhouses' in which we can store an almost infinite amount of knowledge — or at least information — which we can access at the click of a button. Here is what Douglas B Lenat said in an essay, 'From 2001 to *2001*: Common Sense and Mind of HAL':

～

This view is best likened to priming a pump. Visualize your brain as a knowledge pump. Knowledge goes in, gets stored; combined, copied, or whatever; from time to time, you say or write or do things that are, in effect, ways for your brain to emit knowledge. On a good day, the knowledge you give out may be as good or better than the knowledge you put in.

No one expects you to be a productive knowledge pump without training and experience — whether we're talking about playing the piano or tennis, or writing a cheque or a novel, or making a U-turn in a car. You have to invest some learning-and-teaching time and effort before anyone expects you to be competent at a task, let alone to excel at it.

Consider Dr Dave Bowman, mission commander of *Discovery*. His experiences as an engineering or astrophysics student and his astronaut training qualified him to lead the mission. Before that, his high school and undergraduate college prepared him for graduate school and before that, he learned in elementary and middle school the fundamentals he needed for high school. And long before — here we get to some very important stuff indeed — his early experiences as a baby prepared him for kindergarten and first grade. He learned, for instance, to talk and that people generally prepare food in kitchens. He learned that if you leave something, it often remains there, at least for a while. He learned that pouring milk from one glass to another differently shaped glass does not change the total volume of the milk. He learned that there is no air in outer space so he'd better not forget the helmet of his space suit if he's going walking in space. He learned all this — and a million other things.

~

But despite this, all of us have to be increasingly selective about the knowledge 'baggage allowance' we permit ourselves. How much should we carry with us on our life journey, and what should it consist of?

Derek: So what you're talking about is a basic survival kit of knowledge?

Jug: Absolutely. Let's go back to that desert bushman and the New York executive who suddenly exchange places. Suppose they were given a fifteen-minute shopping spree in a knowledge supermarket before being transplanted into an alien environment, what would they put in their shopping baskets? Or in their survival kits, as we called it.

Pythagoras's theorem? Bach's Brandenburg concertos? A history of Chola bronzes? A map of the New York subway system? The names of plants whose roots yield water when squeezed?

Once the bushman succeeded in becoming the Mayor of New York City and the executive established himself as the head honcho of the Kalahari bushmen, they might, respectively, find time and space to learn to play the violin (like Holmes) or read the *Wall Street Journal* to find out if the 'irrational exuberance' of the Dow Jones Index was still going strong.

Derek: So what you're saying is that once we know enough just to live, then we can start living to know?

Jug: You've hit the knowledge nail on the head, Derek. In fact, it helps to think of knowledge as a tree. At the bottom of the tree, closest to its roots, is life-skill related knowledge, concerning the nuts and bolts of one's everyday environment. What is the price of a kilo of rice? If I get so much salary, how should I budget my monthly expenses? Do not stand in the middle of the highway if you do not want to commit suicide. The sun is very strong; cover your head.

Next comes social knowledge. In the survey, the respondents defined this as a requirement 'so that I don't appear dumb when people are talking'. This is knowledge of current affairs, including political developments, gossip, and social trends in fashion, food and life-styles. Tony Blair is the prime minister of Britain. Tom Cruise and Nicole Kidman have separated. Szechwan cuisine has overtaken Cantonese in popularity.

A level above this is career-related knowledge, particularly important to young people about to appear for examinations or job interviews and all those who wish to do well in their fields of work. This kind of knowledge is generally of a specialist nature and requires constant upgradation. What is the latest theory in business management? How far has the human genome project progressed? What are the implications of 3G mobile technology?

And finally we have recreational knowledge, which is know-how that we elect to acquire above and beyond the needs of everyday life and career advancement. Such knowledge, which some call a 'hobby' or just 'time pass', helps to enhance the quality of our leisure time. Be it Indian classical singing, collecting stamps, competing in quizzes or playing the violin, such pursuits of knowledge reflect our personalities, and may be more important to us than we realize. For it is in this knowledge that we can find some knowledge of not only what we are but also of what we hope to become. In a way, it is the knowledge of our dreams.

Derek: The knowledge of dreams. That has a poetic ring.

Jug: It does. A Japanese poet once went to sleep and dreamt he was a butterfly. When he woke up, he wondered if he was really a butterfly who now was dreaming that it was a poet.

CHAPTER 3

How Do We Know What We Know?

Derek: All this stuff about poets and butterflies is great. But how does it get us closer to real knowledge — whatever that might be?

Jug: Good question, Derek. How do we know that what we know is real, and not a dream? What is the bedrock, the unshakable foundation of all our knowledge? This basic question, from which all further questions and their answers flow, was tackled in western philosophy by a French mathematician, scientist and soldier called Rene Descartes who lived from 1596 to 1650. Descartes was a remarkable combination of thinker and man of action. The 'Cartesian system' of 'radical doubt' that he worked out remains a watershed in the history of thought and knowledge, earning him pride of place in the philosophy hall of fame as 'the father of modern western philosophy'.

Derek: Isn't Descàrtes the guy who said, 'I think, therefore I am'? As far as I'm concerned, that's putting Descartes before the horse. Because while everyone quotes his statement, very few people know what it means. What does it mean, anyway, and how did he come to say it?

Jug: Popular lore has it that Descartes, recuperating from a military campaign, sought solitude in a secluded chateau. Here, he locked himself in a room, and began his solitary exploration of the realm of knowledge. He started with the assumption that in order to know anything with certitude we must begin by doubting everything. The chair on which you are sitting as you read this, for instance, need not 'really' exist at all but merely be a figment of your imagination.

Descartes questioned everything that he had been taught to 'know' or believe in: the existence of God, the universe, the room he had confined himself in. When he had cast doubt on everything, he realized that in his very process of doubting, his thinking remained. In order to doubt the existence of everything, I must first exist and I must be able to think. *Cogito ergo sum:* I think, therefore I am. This became the keystone of the great edifice of thought that Descartes was to build and which still casts its shadow on all discussions relating to the basis of knowledge. Here's the man himself:

I suppose ... that all the things which I see are fictitious; I believe that none of those objects which my fallacious memory represents ever existed; I suppose that I possess no senses; I believe that body, figure, extension, motion, and place are merely fictions of my mind. What is there, then, that can be esteemed true? Perhaps this only, that there is absolutely nothing certain.

But how do I know that there is not something different altogether from the objects I have now enumerated, of which it is impossible to entertain the slightest doubt? Is there not a God, or some being, by whatever name I may designate him, who causes these thoughts to arise in my mind? But why suppose such a being, for it may be I myself am capable of producing them? Am I, then, at least not something? But I before denied that I possessed senses or a body; I hesitate, however, for what follows from that? Am I so dependent on the body and the senses that without these I cannot exist? But I had the persuasion that there was absolutely nothing in the world, that there was no sky and no earth, neither minds nor bodies; was I not, therefore, at the same time, persuaded that I did not exist? Far from it; I assuredly existed, since I was persuaded. But there is I know not what being, who is possessed at once of the highest power and the deepest cunning, who is constantly employing all his ingenuity in deceiving me. Doubtless, then, I exist, since I am deceived; and, let him deceive me as he may, he can never bring it about that I am nothing, so long as I shall be conscious that I am something. So that it must, in fine, be maintained, all things being maturely and carefully considered, that this proposition I am, I exist, is necessarily true each time it is expressed by me, or conceived in my mind.

_∽_

Derek: Wow, the guy seems to have got it pretty well figured out.

Jug: He did, but his conclusions had a profound side effect: they caused a split, or dualism, between the knower and what the knower knows, between the mind and the material world, which includes the physical body of the knower as distinct from the incorporeal mind.

This division of separation or an 'inner thought' and an outer reality was to have far reaching consequences in the endless, and often endlessly bewildering, pursuit of knowledge.

Three British thinkers — John Locke (1632-1704), David Hume (1711-1776) and George Berkeley (1685-1753) — were to deepen the divide between 'mind' and 'matter', between the world of our knowledge and the 'real' world 'out there'.

Derek: Weren't these three the founders of what later came to be called British empiricist philosophy?

Jug: Quite right, Derek. Dismissing the Platonic notion that all our knowledge is already within us in the form of Eternal Ideas and only needs to be taken out with the use of reason and imagination, Locke argued that all that we know is derived from what our senses tell

us about the external world and what our experience
has taught us about it. For example, you 'know' that
an apple is an apple because your sense of sight tells
you it is red (or sometimes green), your sense of touch
tells you it is round, and your sense of taste tells you it
is sweet when you bite into it. You can never hope to
know what an apple 'really' is; all you can know are
your own sense perceptions of an apple. Whether or
not these perceptions match with the properties of a
'real' apple is, literally, immaterial to you.

Hume went one step further than Locke. He argued
that our notions of before and after, cause and effect,
on which all our knowledge and thinking is based,
are also dependent on our sensory perceptions and do
not necessarily have any 'reality' in the outer world.
For example, if you see steam rising out of a kettle of
water placed on a fire, you assume that the heat of
the fire is the cause of the steam, which is the effect.
Hume would say the relationship of cause and effect
between fire and steam exists only in your mind. In
the 'real' world, fire and steam are two separate
phenomena unconnected with each other. It is we who
create the illusion of relationship. Not just between
fire and steam but also between all the impressions
received from the outer world by a single self, the 'I'
that we call ourselves. According to Hume, even this
'I' or self lacks any objective reality. Both the outer

world and the inner world are equally 'unreal'.

Berkeley, a bishop, agreed that so-called reality was just an appearance. An apple was not really sweet but only appeared to be sweet to us because of the action of our taste buds. If our sense of taste was chemically changed, the apple would lose its sweetness. But if everything was only appearance, what kept the world going? Bishop Berkeley's answer was simple: the omniscient 'eye of God'. By seeing everything, it conferred reality on everything.

Derek: How does all this square with the view of the world that a modern scientist might have?

Jug: Modern science, which does not necessarily believe in the good bishop's idea of God, has even stranger things to say about 'reality' and our knowledge of it. Modern physics tells us that the world of matter is not really solid and substantial at all but a dancing interplay of molecules. This table that you sit at to eat is not 'really' a table but a rhythm of force fields imperceptible to our senses. Worse is to come. The Nobel Prize-winning German physicist Werner Heisenberg (1901-1976) suggested in his famous 'Uncertainty Principle' that when scientists in a laboratory try to investigate molecular patterns, the very process of investigation alters those patterns. In short, when we try to acquire knowledge about

something, we alter the subject of our knowledge. Then there was Schrodinger and his famous cat.

Derek: I've heard of Dick Whittington's cat. Who's this cat Schrodinger who also had a cat?

Jug: Erwin Schrodinger (1887-1961) literally put the cat among the pigeons of scientific knowledge. In a hypothesis that was to become famous as the 'case of Schrodinger's cat', he postulated a cat which is put inside a closed box. The lid of the box is attached to a randomly operated mechanism which might or might not release a poison gas within the box, killing the cat.

Schrodinger argued that once the box's lid is down we can have no further knowledge of the cat, unless we open the lid — which may or may not result in the cat's death. Since no scientific statement can be made without proof — and since in this case, providing proof of the cat's existence might in fact kill it — the cat in the box, scientifically speaking, is neither alive nor dead but in a state of limbo.

Truly a case of curiosity killing the cat.

CHAPTER 4

True and False Knowledge

Derek: All this talk about cats is making the quest for knowledge seem like a pet shop.

Jug: That it is. And there's more to come. Including snakes.

Derek: You mean like the serpent who tempted Eve with the Fruit of Knowledge in the Garden of Eden?

Jug: Not quite. Hundreds of years before Schrodinger's twilight zone cat called in to question the smug certitude of knowledge, Indian philosophy had done exactly that through Shankara's conundrum of the serpent and the rope. You see something coiled in a dark corner. It could be a poisonous serpent, or only a harmless, useful rope. The effect — whether to call for help, or to pick up the rope for future use — is determined by a cause based on imperfect data (conditioned in this case by your fallible sense of sight) which could be illusory but which will have very real consequences for you. If the 'rope' turns out to be a serpent, you will get bitten; if the 'serpent' turns out to be a rope, you'll become a laughing stock among your friends. False or 'unreal' knowledge can be as effective in shaping our world and our actions as 'real' knowledge, especially since 'unreal' knowledge can be harder to jettison than 'real' knowledge — witness the case of Marco Polo and the unicorn as told by Umberto Eco in *Kant and the Platypus*.

Marco Polo and the Unicorn

Often, when faced with an unknown phenomenon, we react by approximation: we seek that scrap of content, already present in our encyclopedia, which for better or worse seems to account for the new fact. A classic example of this process is to be found in Marco Polo, who saw what we now realize were rhinoceroses on Java. Although he had never seen such animals before, by analogy with other known animals he was able to distinguish the body, the four feet, and the horn. Since his culture provided him with the notion of a unicorn — a quadruped with a horn on its forehead, to be precise — he designated those animals as unicorns. Then, as he was an honest and meticulous chronicler, he hastened to tell us that these unicorns were rather strange — not very good examples of the species, we might say — given that they were not white and slender but had 'the hair of the buffalo' and feet 'like the feet of an elephant.' He went on to give even more detail:

It has one horn in the middle of the forehead — very

thick and large and black. And I tell you that it does no harm to men and beasts with its horn, but only with the tongue and knee, for on its tongue it has very long spines and sharp...It has the top of the head made like a wild boar... It is a very ugly beast to see and unclean. And they are not so as we here say and describe, who say that it lets itself be caught in the lap by a virgin girl: but I tell you that it is quite the contrary of that which we believe that it was.

Marco Polo seems to have made a decision: rather than resegment the content by adding a new animal to the universe of the living, he has corrected the contemporary description of unicorns, so that, if they existed, they would be as he saw them and not as the legend described them. He has modified the intension and left the extension unchanged. Or at least that is what it seems he wanted to do, or in fact did, without bothering his head overmuch regarding taxonomy!

～

Derek: I knew Marco Polo introduced pasta to Italy after his trip to China, where he tasted noodles. I didn't know he invented unicorns as well. But can you give me a more contemporary example of 'unreal' knowledge?

Jug: Sure. In the modern age, false knowledge has been institutionalized in the form of politically sponsored propaganda and made all the more effective by being amplified by mass media. During the Vietnam war, Norman Mailer coined the word 'factoid' to mean a statistic or event cooked up by the propaganda machine and repeated over and over till it was generally accepted as a fact, and made people act accordingly — in this case, made them support the US involvement in Vietnam. The point that Mailer was making was not just political but epistemological, dealing with knowledge and the fruits of knowledge. As Mailer's 'factoids' show, from a seed of false knowledge can spring an only too real and painful bed of thorns.

For example, pro-Nazi historians are even today promoting the factoid that the holocaust never happened and is merely a figment of collective imagnation.

It is often — and rightly — said that knowledge is power. But the reverse is also true, and often dangerously true: that power is knowledge, implying that those who are powerful have the ability to distort and misuse it.

Derek: So knowledge, and its misuse, can be dangerous.

Jug: It certainly can. In George Orwell's *1984* — perhaps the most definitive novel about the dangers of political propaganda and the spread of false knowledge — the citizens of the three enemy states which comprise the world have been taught to talk 'Doublespeak', a 'language' of non-communication in which words like 'love' and 'hate', 'war' and 'peace' have lost all meaning and become interchangeable. History is constantly being obliterated and recreated, like ripples of sand in a windblown desert. With no knowledge of the past or hope for the future, the citizens of *1984* are trapped in the solitary confinement of an illusory present.

Orwell's novel was an indictment of Stalinist Russia. (It is said that he hit upon the title by interposing the last two digits of 1948, when Stalinism was at its height.) Like all totalitarian regimes, Stalinist Russia was, in fact, a fertile breeding ground for 'factoids', which were often disguised as revolutionary scientific discoveries. One of the best known Soviet factoid of this kind was propounded by a biologist, Trofim Lysenko (1898-1976), who claimed that characteristics or knowledge acquired by an organism through experience were genetically passed on to the offspring. For instance, if a particular non-aquatic creature somehow learnt to swim, this acquired ability would be inherited by its progeny who would also be able to swim. Lysenko's theories , which had a lot in common with similar ideas earlier suggested by Jean Baptiste Pierre Antoine de Monet de Lamarck (1744-1829), contradicted Charles Darwin's universally accepted theory that evolutionary traits are not directly transmitted through heredity but come about through a process of natural selection in which the fittest individuals — those most in tune with their environment — survive and reproduce themselves while the weakest — those out of tune with their environment — get phased out.

Derek: So how did this Lysenko's theories gain political respectability?

Jug: Simple. Lysenko's proposition suited Stalin who wanted to propagate the idea of a 'New Man' who would come into being thanks to the political and economic environment of Communism and who would change the evolutionary history of the planet. Though Lysenko's theories — including his principal 'discovery' of 'vernalized' wheat which would radically change agricultural patterns — were never satisfactorily put to the test in a laboratory, his critics were made victims of political persecution, and at least one was sent off to the Gulag on the trumped-up charge that he was a British spy.

Derek: Not a very scientific approach, was it?

Jug: It certainly wasn't. Lysenkoism is believed to have set back by decades Soviet research in the crucial areas of genetics and bio-technology. But this was by no means the first 'factoid' to act as a stumbling block to progress. For over 1500 years western civilization

believed (together with Sherlock Holmes) that the sun moved around the earth, as propounded by the Alexandrian astronomer Ptolemy in AD 140. The first person to challenge Ptolemy was Copernicus in the sixteenth century. But even he was discreet enough to do so only in a posthumously published work. Galileo (1564-1642) who supported the Copernican view of the universe was persecuted by the Inquisition and formally had to recant his 'heresy'. Or should we say 'hear-say', in keeping with the genealogy of 'factoids'?

Derek: Tough job, being a scientist in those days.

Jug: It still is. Galileo died in the year that Isaac Newton, the 'father of modern science', was born. Newton's ideas on gravitation and the movement of celestial bodies became the official writ for 200 years till they in turn were called into question by Einstein's theory of relativity: space and time are curved; our 'knowledge' of 'reality' is relative to where we are located on the curve. Since then, molecular physics has spawned a fantastical menagerie of elementary particles (including tachyons which supposedly go faster than light and so, hypothetically, can travel backward in time) which suggest that the cosmos, or at least our knowledge of it, is a continuously changing three-ring circus. In which we are the eternal clowns, in our unceasing efforts to gain full knowledge of it, finally and forever.

Derek: So now we have the 'circus of knowledge'. Or should that be the 'circle of knowledge'?

Jug: Perhaps both. Confronted with the question how 'real' is 'reality', science has adopted an idiom suspiciously similar to that of mysticism — or of comedy. As Gary Zulov says in his book on the new physics, *The Dancing Wu-li Masters:* 'Reality is what we take to be true. What we take to be true is what we believe. What we believe is based upon our precepts. What we perceive depends on what we look for. What we look for depends on what we perceive. What we perceive determines what we believe. What we believe determines what we take to be true. What we take to be true is our reality.'

Or, as Groucho Marx almost put it: I would not care to join any reality which would have me as a member.

CHAPTER 5

Zen and the Art of Paradox Maintenance

Derek: Hey, just hang on a sec. We ended the last chapter with you paraphrasing Groucho Marx to the effect that you would not care to join any reality which would have you as a member. But if we're not part of reality, what are we part of then?

Jug: Perhaps we could be part of a reality which lies beyond what we think is the real. Let me tell you a story.

The emperor of China was a connoisseur of horses and boasted that he had the best stable in the world. This was thanks largely to the efforts of his Master of the Horse, who had an uncanny ability to locate and identify the finest of animals. After many years of dedicated service to the emperor, during which he travelled all over the land to find superlative mounts for the imperial stable, the ageing Master requested that he be allowed to retire. The emperor reluctantly agreed, on condition that the Master got and trained a suitable replacement for himself.

The Master selected a young man, a village yokel,

and began to train him in the fine art of judging horseflesh. Finally, the Master declared himself satisfied and the novice was sent off to bring back, as a test, the 'most excellent mount in the world' for the emperor.

The young man set out on his search for the 'most excellent mount'. Months passed, and a message was received from him that he had at last found such an animal, a black stallion. The emperor and his court waited in eager anticipation for the return of the young man with the horse. When they did return however, the entire court was aghast. For the black stallion, supposed to be the 'most excellent mount in the world', turned out to be a white mare. Enraged, the emperor sent for the old Master of the Horse. 'You told me this young fellow was an expert judge of horses. Yet now we see that he cannot even tell the difference between a black stallion and a white mare. What sort of a fool have you selected?' thundered the emperor. When he heard this, the Master of the Horse smiled with satisfaction. 'You say he can't tell the difference between a black stallion and a white mare? I knew that as my pupil, he had learnt a lot, but even I did not think he could have learnt so much. Ride the horse, Sire. I am certain it will prove to be the most excellent mount in the world.'

The story goes that the emperor did ride the horse.

And the horse did indeed turn out to be the most excellent in the world.

Derek: Wow, I wish I had a horse master like that. The horses I back at the races always come in last.

Jug: Maybe what you need to do is study Zen to know your horses better. Because Zen suggests that there is knowledge beyond knowledge, an uncommon wisdom that lies beyond what is commonly accepted as common sense. This 'uncommon sense' has at different times been given many different names: intuition, Zen, lateral thinking.

Derek: And here I thought the Zen was just a small car with a huge advertising budget.

Jug: It's ironic that Maruti Suzuki should introduce a car called the Zen in India, because India exported the original Zen to Japan. Zen, derived from the Sanskrit word 'dhyan' meaning mind or thought, was introduced to Japan in the eighth century, via China, by the Indian sage Bodhidharma, the so-called 'barbarian from the west'. This unusual philosopher used the most unconventional means — including kicking his disciples downstairs — to overcome the barriers and traps that reason often sets for itself. Zen fights shy of being defined as a religion, or a school of philosophy, or mysticism or even a mental discipline. In fact, Zen sometimes refers to itself as 'non-sense'. Zen is not a destination but a journey, not a product but a process. It is an attitude, a way of looking at things out of the corner of the eye of our mind, a shift in perspective that makes the seeming contradictions which baffled us disappear on their own.

Derek: But if Zen defines itself as 'non-sense', then how does one go about systematically learning it? In other words, how does one make sense out of non-sense?

Jug: Zen pupils are asked 'koans' or riddles to which there are no logical answers: You know the sound of two hands clapping. But what is the sound of one hand clapping?

The 'koan' is a key to unlocking a mind-set, which has been conditioned to see everything in yes/no, either/or, and true/false terms by which we define the world of our concepts. But our concepts themselves teach us that there are some concepts which cannot be defined; they can only be participated in. Heisenberg's Principle of Indeterminacy — which says that by asking to know the truth of something we change the nature, or truth, of what we seek to know — is one such concept. The sound of one hand clapping is another. There can be no 'answer' to the question of

the one-handed handclap. But there certainly can be a response. For example, a Zen pupil asked this unanswerable riddle could respond in any of a number of ways: by getting up and walking out of the room, or perhaps by asking the teacher the counter-question: 'Why do you differentiate between sound and silence?'

Gauging the response of the pupil, the teacher would decide whether the pupil had learnt how to overcome paradox: not by sidestepping it, but by astride-stepping it. By getting over it through the creative power of lateral thinking. Making a seeming 'problem' stop being a problem by looking out at it from a new perspective.

Derek: I'm neither a Zen Buddhist nor a theoretical physicist. So what sort of perspective would I have on paradoxes? Would I even recognize one if it was introduced to me by first name?

Jug: Sure you would. You don't have to be a Zen Buddhist or a theoretical physicist like Heisenberg to come across paradoxes and discover the need to astride-step them. A paradox is not an either/or or a true/false concept but an either/either or a true/true concept in which two equally valid truths seem to contradict each other. An example: what happens when an irresistible force meets an immovable object?

If a force is irresistible, by definition it must be

able to move any object, even an immovable one. But if an object is immovable, by definition it cannot be moved, not even by an irresistible force.

Here's another one: can God, who is omnipotent (i.e. capable of doing anything He wants to) build a wall so high that He cannot jump across? If he can build such a wall then He is not omnipotent because then He will not be able to jump over it; if He can jump over it He is not omnipotent because He has not built an unjumpable wall.

You can make your own paradox. On side A of a sheet of paper write, 'The statement on the other side of this sheet is true'. Turn the sheet over to side B and write, 'The statement on the other side of this sheet is false'. Now go mad trying to figure out what's true, what's false, what's what. If A is true, then B is true when it says A is false. But if A is false, then when it says that B is true it is being false. So B is false, when B says that A is false A is really true. So that...

Derek: Hey, that's neat. I must pull this trick the next time I'm at a party.

Jug: Be my guest. But paradoxes are more than just mental party tricks. Heisenberg and other modern physicists believe that paradoxes are inexplicable 'glitches' in the universe, or at least in the way in which we apprehend the universe. Long before

Heisenberg, the German transcendentalist thinker Immanuel Kant (1724-1804) showed in his *Critique of Pure Reason* that paradoxes were lodged in the texture of rational thought itself. Though we have *a priori* knowledge of the world, this knowledge does not apply to the actual world or the thing in itself, but only to our hypothesis of the real world. Or, as he put it:

⌐⌐⌐

In metaphysical speculations it has always been assumed that all our knowledge must conform to objects; but every attempt from this point of view to extend our knowledge of objects *a priori* by means of conceptions has ended in failure. The time has now come to ask, whether better progress may not be made by supposing that objects must conform to our knowledge. Plainly this would better agree with the avowed aim of metaphysics, to determine the nature of objects *a priori*, or before they are actually presented. Our suggestion is similar to that of Copernicus in astronomy, who, finding it impossible to explain the movements of the heavenly bodies on the supposition that they turned round the spectator, tried whether he might succeed better by supposing the spectator to revolve and the stars to remain at rest. Let us make a similar experiment in metaphysics with perception. If it were really necessary for our perception to conform to the nature of objects, I do not see how we could know anything of it *a priori*; but if the sensible object must conform to the constitution of our faculty of perception, I see no difficulty in the matter. Perception, however, can become knowledge only if it is related in some way to the object which it determines. Now here again I may suppose, either that the conceptions through which I effect that determination conform to the objects, or that the objects, in other words the experience in which alone the objects are known, conform to conceptions. In the former case, I fall into the same perplexity as before, and fail to explain how such conceptions can be known *a priori*. In the latter case, the outlook is more hopeful. For, experience is itself a mode of knowledge which implies intelligence, and intelligence has a rule of its own, which must be an *a priori* condition of all knowledge of objects presented to it. To this rule, as expressed in *a priori* conceptions, all objects of experience must necessarily conform, and with it they must agree.

⁓

Try this one. Take an infinite number. The number perforce, has to be either odd or even. Divide the number in half. If the original number were even, you'd have two identical but separate infinities, which is unthinkable. If the number were odd, you'd have an even more unthinkable proposition: two infinities, with one infinity being larger than the other.

Derek: All these paradoxes sound like Hulk Hogan putting half-nelsons on us. How do we manage to get anything done at all? Why is this Kant of yours such a can't-do kind of guy?

Jug: Actually, he was a pretty can-do fellow. In fact, he rescued us from the quicksand of paradox. Kant evolved a system of ethics based on the 'categorical imperative': act as if your every action can become a universal maxim. In other words, do unto others what you would have them do unto you!

The contemporary advertising slogan for Niké sportswear puts it even more succinctly: Just do it. Horseman, ride by. And don't worry and waffle too much about whether you're riding a black stallion or a white mare. So long as it is a most excellent mount.

CHAPTER 6

The Never-ending Universe of Knowledge

Derek: Well, if you're saying that a white mare and a black stallion can be interchangeable, then it seems that there's no end to what we *don't* know about knowledge.

Jug: So it would seem. Because were we to get to the end of knowledge, would that also be the end of *us*? Are we and our quest for knowledge the only way for the universe to find out what it doesn't know about itself?

In an Arthur C Clarke fable, an American computerologist is invited to a remote Buddhist monastery in the Himalayas for a special project. The abbot of the monastery explains to him that according to scriptural lore, there were nine billion names of God and the purpose of all existence was to enumerate them. In the pre-computer age, such a task was unthinkable. But now with the use of supercomputers, such as the one they had in the monastery, it should be possible to put on a single programme all of the nine billion names of God.

The computerologist begins inputting data, collecting and collating all the names of God. The weeks and months pass and finally the project is complete: all the nine billion names of God have been logged in. The programmer goes out to break the good news to the abbot who is standing on the ramparts of the monastery. 'It's done,' says the computerologist excitedly. 'I know,' replies the abbot calmly, and silently points to the heavens where, one by one, the stars are going out like extinguished lamps as the cosmos — having completed the work for which it was created — folds up like a discarded computer printout.

The moral of the story is that we are nothing more, or less, than a quest for knowledge. When that quest ends, we ourselves end.

Derek: In effect, what you're saying is that knowledge feeds on itself and the more it feeds, the hungrier it gets?

Jug: That's right. Knowledge is a process, not an end product; a journey, not a destination. Let's go back to our Kalahari bushman and the Wall Street tycoon who have traded places. Once ensconced in his corner office overlooking Manhattan's Battery Park, the bushman will not stop his process of learning, his quest for more and more knowledge. Having mastered the skill of financial manipulation, he will find he must familiarize himself with the protocol of power lunches, which wines to order with which course, what paintings to acquire for his art collection. Similarly, the Wall Street magnate turned bushman tribal chief will not cease educating himself in his new environment. Learning how to make and consolidate alliances with a neighboring tribe, which will prove mutually beneficial. Figuring out if the 'random walk' theory of selecting financial scrip can be translated into finding waterholes in the desert. Seeing if Drucker's mantras on corporate management can be applied to maximize the efficiency of hunting-gathering functions.

Derek: So what you're basically saying is that knowledge is a perpetual motion machine.

Jug: Almost right, Derek. Actually, knowledge is a perpetual *notion* machine. It generates itself and cannot, and should not, ever come to a stop. But precisely because of the constant challenge that the ever-receding, unreachable horizon of knowledge poses to the mind, thinkers of many cultures and eras have tried to lay frameworks of knowledge which would define and limit knowledge for all time. At least in theory.

Derek: Isn't that rather like a quiz master saying the only legitimate questions that can be asked are those from his book?

Jug: An apt analogy, Derek. But for quiz master read religious believer, who believes that his God-revealed Book has the final say on all things. One such advocate for divine omniscience was the German mathematician, diplomat and theologian Gottfried Wilhelm Leibniz (1646-1716). A product of the turmoil of Europe's Thirty-Year War, Leibniz longed for peace and stability. He strove for these goals with a robust optimism backed by the power of a vigorous intellect. As a diplomatist, he drew up blueprints for a united Europe, 300 years ahead of his time. As a mathematician, he devised differential calculus, as an analytical tool with which to investigate all phenomena. But it was as a theologian that he proposed his grandest concept, that of a 'pre-ordained harmony', which underlies everything and ensures that ours is 'the best of possible worlds'.

~

It is well to bear in mind that God does nothing out of order. Therefore, that which passes for extraordinary is so only with regard to a particular order established among the created things, for as regards the universal order, everything conforms to it. This is so true that not only does nothing occur in this world which is absolutely irregular, but it is even impossible to conceive of such an occurrence.

Because, let us suppose for example that someone jots down a quantity of points upon a sheet of paper helter skelter, as do those who exercise the ridiculous art of geomancy; now I say that it is possible to find a geometrical line whose concept shall be uniform and constant, that is, in accordance with a certain formula, and which line at the same time shall pass through all of those points, and in the same order in which the hand jotted them down; also if a continuous line be traced, which is now straight, now circular, and now of any other description, it is possible to find a mental equivalent, a formula or an equation common to all the points of this line by virtue of which formula the changes in the direction of the line must occur.

There is no instance of a face whose contour does not form part of a geometric line and which cannot be traced entire by a certain mathematical motion. But when the formula is very complex, that which conforms to it passes for irregular. Thus we may say that in whatever manner God might have created the world, it would always have been regular and in a certain order. God, however, has chosen the most perfect, that is to say the one which is at the same time the simplest in hypotheses and the richest in phenomena, as might be the case with a geometric line, whose construction was easy, but whose properties and effects were extremely remarkable and of great significance. I use these comparisons to picture a certain imperfect resemblance to the divine wisdom, and to point out that which may at least raise our minds to conceive in some sort what cannot otherwise be expressed.

～

Jug: According to Leibniz, the world and everything

in it, including us human beings, consisted of atomic 'metaphysical' particles, which he called 'monads'. Monads were autonomous and informed with consciousness and interacted with each other according to the laws of a 'pre-ordained harmony' which underpinned everything, from the motion of a single wave on the boundless ocean to the rise and fall of mighty empires. If one could establish the location and direction of each and every monad, said Leibniz, it should be possible to apply the principles of calculus and determine not only the course of all future events but also those of the past. In short, one would be able to know everything there was to know. But since God was the only one who was in a position to know exactly where and what each and every monad was up to at any given moment, such knowledge remained out of the practical grasp of humanity. At least for the time being. Heisenberg, who was to propound his Indeterminacy Principle some 250 years later, would have changed 'for the time being' to 'for all time'.

Derek: You mean Leibniz saw God as the supreme mathematician?

Jug: In a way, yes. But the trouble is that mathematicians can sometimes ask questions they themselves can't answer. An example of this is Kurt Godel and his famous loop, which can tie the universe of numbers into a Gordian knot, as Douglas R Hofstadt demonstrates in *Godel, Escher, Bach: An Eternal Golden Braid:*

～

In its absolutely barest form, Godel's discovery involves the translation of an ancient paradox in philosophy into mathematical terms. That paradox is the so-called Epimenides paradox, or liar paradox. Epimenides was a Cretan who made one immortal statement: 'All Cretans are liars'. A sharper version of the statement is simply 'I am lying': or, 'This statement is false'. It is that last version which I will usually mean when I speak of the Epimenides paradox. It is a statement which rudely violates the usually assumed dichotomy of statements into true and false, because if you tentatively think it is true, then it immediately backfires on you and makes you think it is false. But once you've decided it is false, a similar backfiring returns you to the idea that it must be true. Try it!

The Epimenides paradox is a one-step Strange Loop, like Escher's Print Gallery. But what does it have to do with mathematics? That is what Godel discovered. His idea was to use mathematical reasoning in exploring mathematical reasoning itself. This notion of making mathematics 'introspective' proved to be enormously powerful, and perhaps its richest implication was the one Godel found: Godel's Incompleteness Theorem.

Godel's Theorem appears as Proposition VI in his 1931 paper, 'On Formally Undecidable Propositions in Principia Mathematica and Related Systems I.' It states:

To every w-consistent recursive class k of formulae there correspond recursive class-signs r, such that neither v Gen r nor Neg (v Gen r) belongs to Flg (k) (where v is the free variable of r).

Actually, it was in German, and perhaps you feel that it might as well be in German anyway. So here is a paraphrase in more normal English:

All consistent axiomatic formulations of number theory include undecidable propositions.

This is the pearl.

In this pearl it is hard to see a Strange Loop. That is because the Strange Loop is buried in the oyster — the proof. The proof of Godel's Incompleteness Theorem hinges upon the writing of a self-referential mathematical statement, in the same way as the Epimenides paradox is a self-referential statement of language. But whereas it is very simple to talk about language in language, it is not at all easy to see how a statement about numbers can talk about itself ...

Godel's Theorem had an electrifying effect upon logicians, mathematicians, and philosophers interested in the foundations of mathematics, for it showed that no fixed system, no matter how complicated, could represent the complexity of the whole numbers: 0, 1, 2, 3 ...

⁓

As you can see, Godel's loop and similar mental roller-coasters suggest that the very process of acquiring knowledge contains strange twists and turns, which defy knowledge.

Derek: Since we're talking maths, isn't it true that Bertrand Russell's great work, *Principia Mathematica*, remained incomplete because he couldn't come to a mathematically satisfactory conclusion?

Jug: That's right. One of the greatest thinkers of modern times, Bertrand Russell (1872-1970) stumbled upon one of these inexplicable whorls or warps in the seemingly seamless fabric of thought while working on his magnum opus in collaboration with A N Whitehead. What seemed at first a simple problem in mathematical logic (Imagine a series of 'sets', of numbers, objects, concepts such as KQ. Now imagine a set, which includes all other sets. Can this all-inclusive set itself be included in the scheme of sets or not?) swiftly turned out to be a nightmare from which the mathematician-philosopher feared that he would never awaken to greet the 'glad, confident morning' of rational thought again. In his own words:

∿

At first I supposed that I should be able to overcome the contradiction quite easily, and that probably there was some trivial error in the reasoning. Gradually however, it became clear that this was not the case. Burali-Forti had already discovered a similar contradiction, and it turned out on logical analysis that there was an affinity with the ancient Greek contradiction about Epimenides the Cretan, who said that all Cretans are liars. It seemed unworthy of a grown man to spend his time on such trivialities, but what was I to do? There was something wrong since such contradictions were unavoidable on ordinary premises. Trivial or not, the matter was a challenge. Throughout the latter half of 1901 I supposed the solution would be easy, but by the end of that time I had concluded that it was a big job. I therefore decided to finish *The Principles of Mathematics*, leaving the solution in abeyance. In the autumn Alys and I went back to Cambridge, as I had been invited to give two terms' lectures on mathematical logic. These lectures contained the outline of *Principia Mathematica*, but without any method of dealing with the contradictions. The summers of 1903 and 1904 we spent at Churt and Tilford. I made a practice of wandering about the common every night from eleven until one, by which means I came to know the three different noises made by nightjars. (Most people only know one.) I was trying hard to solve the contradictions mentioned above. Every morning I would sit down before a blank sheet of paper. Throughout the day, with a brief interval for lunch, I would stare at the blank sheet. Often when evening came it was still empty. We spent our winters in London, and during the winters I did not attempt to work, but the two summers of 1903 and 1904 remain in my mind as a period of complete intellectual deadlock. It was clear to me that I could not get on without solving the contradictions, and I was determined that no difficulty should turn me aside from the completion of *Principia Mathematica*, but it seemed quite likely that the whole of the rest of my life might be consumed in looking at the blank sheet of paper. What made it the more annoying was that the contradictions were trivial, and that my time was spent in considering matters that seemed unworthy of serious attention.

Derek: Tell me Jug, could it be that there is a basic graininess, a 'sludge', not just in the way our minds work but in the nature of the universe itself, which makes knowledge ultimately unknowable?

Jug: It could be more than just sludge, Derek. It could be a quicksand, which sucks in all the preconceptions we have about the knowable universe. In 1964, A J Bell, a physicist working in Switzerland, formulated a theorem which mathematically 'proved' that a pair of identically polarized elementary particles — such as photons, say — when separated from each other like separated Siamese twins and sent to opposite ends of the universe would be able to 'communicate', i.e. exchange knowledge, with each other instantaneously. Bell's theorem, considered by many physicists and mathematicians to be the most challenging proposition of science, 'disproves' the fundamental law of the universe that nothing can travel faster than the speed of light. Apparently knowledge can and does — and in so doing confounds itself.

Is knowledge, then, the nine billionth and first name of God?

CHAPTER 7

The Third Wave and the Knowledge Worker

Derek: OK, now that we have some idea what knowledge is, let's talk about the role it plays in everyday life.

Vikas Singh: Right. One of the striking features of our times is the fact that knowledge has become a commodity. It was something only a few academicians and the clergy bothered with earlier, but now most people are actively pursuing it. The result is what we could call the democratization of opportunity. Think of it this way. In feudal, even industrial, societies, it was hard to get very far if you weren't born right. In the knowledge economy, though, you just have to be born bright.

And that's changing a whole lot of other things. For example, the 'capital' in capitalism used to mean production equipment and cash. Today, it increasingly refers to the intangible knowledge that resides in people's minds. Earlier, people who worked for an organization were considered employees; today, they're increasingly seen as associates. After all, as Peter Drucker has pointed out: 'Once beyond the apprentice stage, knowledge workers must know more about their job than their boss does — or else they are no good at all.'

Derek: But didn't Drucker also say the IT revolution doesn't amount to much?

Vikas: Not really. Drucker's argument is that societies and economies only change when the focus shifts from 'T' (technology) to 'I' (information). He says there have been four such information revolutions in history. The first one was the invention of writing, the second the invention of the written book. The third was set off by Gutenberg's invention of the printing press and of movable type between 1450 and 1455, and by the invention of engraving around the same time. And the fourth is the one we're living through today.

Drucker's point is that the third information revolution was every bit as sweeping in its impact as the present one. At the time that Gutenberg introduced the press, the information industry was probably Europe's biggest employer. It consisted of hundreds of monasteries, housing large numbers of highly skilled monks — each of whom laboured all day copying books by hand.

Fifty years later, the monks were unemployed, replaced by a few craftsmen. The printing revolution turned books from a luxury available to only a few to a mass medium. Popular literature was born as a result. So was modern education. Unlike earlier universities, which focused on the study of theology, the new universities were built around 'lay' disciplines: law, medicine, mathematics, science.

Printing also made possible the Protestant Reformation. At least, Drucker thinks so. Earlier reformation efforts had received enthusiastic popular response, but could not travel faster than the hand-written word. So, they were easily localized and suppressed. But Martin Luther's famous ninety-five theses, which he nailed to a church door, were quickly printed and distributed first through Germany, and then throughout Europe.

Finally, printing provided navigators and explorers with new, more reliable maps, making possible the entire age of discovery, the great Portuguese voyages, and Columbus's quest for America — and all of us are still living with the consequences today.

Derek: Point taken. So how does Drucker fit into the context of today's knowledge economy?

Vikas: Well, he coined the term 'knowledge worker', way back in 1959, to talk about the worker who would work with his or her mind, not just their hands. Different people have subsequently used varying words to describe the same concept. For example, Robert Reich prefers to talk about 'symbolic analysts' — people who deal with numbers and ideas, problems and words. They include financial analysts, consultants, architects, lawyers, doctors, managers and, ahem, journalists. Basically, intelligence is their source of power and influence.

Derek: Before we go further, wasn't it Henry Ford who said his problem was that he wanted to hire just a pair of hands for the assembly line, but minds came along as well?

Vikas: True, and it's no coincidence that cowboys and factory workers were colloquially called 'hands'. Still, Drucker, being a congenital contrarian, loves to point out that the assembly line marked probably the first time knowledge had ever been applied to manual work. Poets who wrote about the glories of farming had never so much as touched a sickle, Karl Marx wrote about the industrial proletariat without having ever operated a machine.

Frederick Winslow Taylor (1856-1915) was the first

one to break down a task into a series of constituent motions, and then suggest the most efficient sequence and tools. He showed that there is no such thing as 'skill' in manual work, only simple, repetitive motions. They are made productive by knowledge — of how the motions should be organized and executed. Till Taylor came along, there was no concept of labour productivity. Any increase in output came about through new tools, methods, or technology. But the manual worker's productivity was assumed to be a constant. Taylor's path-breaking work saw the manual worker's productivity rising by three per cent every year — a fifty-fold rise in one century. In Drucker's words: 'On this achievement rests *all* the economic and social gains of the twentieth century. The productivity of the manual worker has created what we now call "developed" economies.'

Drucker argues that every method during these last 100 years that has had the slightest success in raising the productivity of manual workers — and with it their real wages — has been based on Taylor's principles. That's true of the Japanese 'Kaizen', 'just-in-time' as well as W Edward Deming's Total Quality Management (TQM).

Derek: I suppose one could qualify that by saying

that the more knowledge was applied to manufacturing, the better the results.

Vikas: Exactly, Derek. Japanese carmakers told workers it was all right to use their minds as well as their hands and gave them a much bigger role in the quality maintenance process. After taking a severe pounding, Detroit was forced to follow suit. But if you accept Drucker's argument that all this is just an extension of Taylor's principles of task analysis and industrial engineering, then it becomes easy to understand why he insists that Taylor's 'scientific management' is the one American philosophy that has swept the world. The only worldwide philosophy that could compete with Taylor's was Marxism. Taylor triumphed, by ensuring ever-increasing productivity and economic growth.

The new challenge for societies in the Third Wave will be to sustain relentless productivity growth among knowledge workers and technologists — let's club them together as tech-knowledgists — people who do both knowledge-based and manual work, like surgeons or even computer-operators. But what are the factors that one will have to take care of? Let's hear it straight from Drucker:

⌒

SIX major factors determine knowledge-worker productivity:
1. Knowledge worker productivity demands that we ask the question: '*what is the task?*'
2. It demands that we impose the responsibility for their productivity on the individual knowledge workers themselves. Knowledge workers *have* to manage themselves. They have to have *autonomy.*
3. Continuing innovation has to be part of the work, the task and the responsibility of knowledge workers.
4. Knowledge work requires continuous learning on the part of the knowledge worker, but equally continuous teaching on the part of the knowledge worker.
5. Productivity of the knowledge worker is not – at least not primarily – a matter of the *quantity* of output. *Quality* is at least as important.
6. Finally, knowledge worker productivity requires that the knowledge worker is both seen and treated as an 'asset' rather than a 'cost'. It requires that knowledge workers *want* to work for the organization in preference to all other opportunities.

    … In most knowledge work, quality is not a minimum and a restraint. Quality is the essence of the output. In judging the performance of a teacher, we do not ask how many students there can be in his or her class. We ask how many students learn anything – and that's a quality question. In appraising the performance of a medical laboratory, the question of how many tests it can run through its machines is quite secondary to the question of how many test results are valid and reliable. And this is true even for the work of the file clerk.

    Productivity of knowledge work, therefore, has to aim first at obtaining quality – and not minimum quality but optimum if not maximum quality. Only then can one ask: 'what is the volume, the quantity of work'.

⌢

Derek: Neat. But let's backtrack for a moment. You spoke about the 'Third Wave'. You're quoting Alvin Toffler, aren't you?

Vikas: Right. In a bestseller called *The Third Wave*, published in 1980, American futurist Alvin Toffler described three periods of economic evolution. The first was the agricultural wave, which lasted from 800 BC to the mid-eighteenth century. This was followed by the industrial wave, which lasted until the late twentieth century. Finally, there was the information wave, which began in the 1960s and will last for many decades to come. The first wave was driven by physical labour, the second by machines and blue-collar workers, and the third by infotech and knowledge workers.

Some people might argue that human resources will become less important in the era of information technology. Not really. As Drucker is fond of pointing out, 'knowing how a typewriter works does not make you a writer'. Now that knowledge is taking the place of capital as the driving force in organizations worldwide, it is all too easy to confuse data with

knowledge and infotech with information. But the fact is, you still need someone to make sense of information — and that's where knowledge comes into the picture.

I think that sums up what we need to know about the rise of the knowledge worker. Of course, that's just part of a much larger topic, 'knowledge management'. But that's another story — actually, another chapter.

CHAPTER 8

Managing Knowledge: Know Why and Know How

Derek: You were speaking about knowledge management earlier. But what's so complex about it? Set up a research lab, give it good funding, get patents. Big deal!

Vikas: Well, that would be fine for intellectual assets, but knowledge isn't quite the same thing.

Derek: So go ahead, define knowledge.

Vikas: Well, as Tony and Jeremy Hope have pointed out, 'Knowledge itself is a fuzzy concept concerned with human cognition and awareness. Knowing a fact is little different from knowing a skill, but knowing how someone (perhaps a competitor or customer) might react to a piece of information requires human intuition and judgement. It is this unique combination of context, memory and cognitive process that separates human knowledge from any other form (such as knowledge-based systems).'

Derek: Phew, this is beginning to sound like an MBA course lecture.

Vikas: Maybe it's time B-schools started handing out MKAs – Masters of Knowledge Administration. And the first chapter in any textbook on the subject should deal with the four levels of knowledge.

Derek: And what might those be?

Vikas: According to James Brian Quinn, Philip Anderson and Sydney Finkelstein, the four levels of knowledge are:

1) Cognitive knowledge (know-what) derived from basic training and certification. This is what you might learn from books.

2) Advanced skill (know-how), which translates book learning into effective execution. In other words, theory applied to real life.

3) Systems understanding (know-why), which builds on the first two and leads to highly trained intuition. This is why, in your home town, you know exactly where to go for the best second-hand books or the best cup of coffee.

4) Self-motivated activity (care-why), which drives creative groups to outperform groups with greater physical or financial resources.

Derek: How would you define intellectual assets, then?

Vikas: Intellectual assets (or capital) are a little easier to define. According to Tony and Jeremy Hope, they come in three types.

1) Human capital or competencies: these include the experience, skills and capabilities of people.
2) Structural or internal capital: these include patents, trademarks and copyright; the store of knowledge in databases and customer lists; and the design and capability of information systems.
3) Market-based or external capital: these include the profitability and loyalty of customers and the strength of brands, licences and franchises.

Derek: OK, I could define one of my intellectual assets as my team of researchers who are constantly supplying me with quiz questions and building databases.

Vikas: Actually, a quiz is a very good analogy for knowledge management, which has broadly two aspects: learning new things and disseminating that learning.

Derek: Speaking of quizzes, can you tell me the name of India's first chief knowledge officer?

Vikas: I give up. You tell me.

Derek: Tut tut. You really should read *The Economic Times*. Hemant Manohar of KPMG became India's first chief knowledge officer three years ago, according to an article in *Corporate Dossier*. Since then, knowledge management is increasingly catching on in corporate India. Infosys has a principal knowledge manager, V P Kochikar. Consulting firm Accenture has built a team of eighteen knowledge managers and looks upon 'KM' as an 'exportable speciality'.

But to return to our subject, I'm sure you're just itching to tell me about some theory on acquiring and disseminating knowledge.

Vikas: Thanks for the invitation. The Hopes list learning by experimentation, past experience (especially failures), the experience of others and acquisition of top individuals, occasionally even whole businesses, as sources of knowledge.

Dorothy Leonard-Barton studied American company Chaparral Steel and said there were four primary learning activities which create and control the knowledge necessary for current and future operations. Three are internally focused: creative problem solving (to produce current products), implementing and integrating new methodologies and tools (to enhance internal operations) and formal and informal experimentation (to build capabilities for the future). The final activity involves importing expertise from outside.

There's also knowledge from external sources like suppliers, partners, customers and other (often unconnected) organizations. Knowledge can be shared between companies, particularly in joint ventures. Then of course, there's the process of benchmarking, which involves looking at best practices of companies well known for excellence in particular processes.

Derek: But tell me, even after it's acquired, does all this knowledge get used?

Vikas: That's one of the biggest challenges for knowledge managers. Tony and Jeremy Hope lament that all too often, knowledge is locked away inside departments and business units. This knowledge is fiercely protected, not just from competitors, but even from colleagues in other departments. That's got to be one of the worst aspects of turf wars. As a result, an organization can often resemble nothing so much as a series of isolated islands of knowledge.

Derek: So how does one go about linking these islands of knowledge?

Vikas: There are two schools of thought on that one: the information school — let's call it the bulletin board method — and the behavioural school, or the get-together method, which is what we're using right now.

Derek: Let's hear about the bulletin-board method?

Vikas: The information school believes that knowledge is a resource to be captured, analysed, coded and deployed for competitive advantage. The basic problem is to break down barriers to knowledge sharing. And the emphasis is on designing systems to make knowledge readily accessible. So, you would share information by putting it up on a bulletin board at a place where people congregate, like maybe the coffee machine. In the case of organizations, they use knowledge-sharing networks and intranets.

Derek: But surely building knowledge-based systems alone does not necessarily ensure that people will use them?

Vikas: Bang on, Derek. Beyond a point, computer networking alone won't suffice. You also have to ensure human networking. Alan M Webber points out the importance of conversations. According to him, it is conversations, not rank or title or trappings of power that determine who is literally and figuratively 'in the loop'. At consultancy firm McKinsey, a director of knowledge management supervises a network dedicated to providing a 'marketplace of readily accessible ideas'. On-call consultants are available on a rotational basis to host conversations with or between staff members who are looking for ideas.

Derek: Fine. What about the behavioural school?

Vikas: The behavioural school believes learning is disseminated by winning the hearts and minds of people. Edgar Schein of the MIT Center for Organizational Learning has observed three broad but distinct subcultures in organizations. The first group, the operator culture, says people are an organization's most important asset and work more effectively in teams than individually. The second group — the engineering culture — sees people as problems who get in the way of elegant solutions. And the third group — the executive culture — is basically focused on financial results.

Each of the three subcultures has learned to tolerate the others, but sometimes their differences can erupt. For example, during a recessionary period, members of the executive culture may decree a reduction in costs. The 'engineering' group may say it should be done by laying off people, rather than reducing spending on machinery. And the 'operators' may say, 'hold on, let's all take a pay cut rather than sacking anyone'. Running in parallel (and sometimes cutting across) these subcultures are communities of practice.

Derek: Explain this new piece of jargon, please.

Vikas: Sure. Tony and Jeremy Hope coined the term to describe small groups of people, cutting across formal departments, who share some common values and generally get the important work done. They are not necessarily an official unit. But they are bound together by a shared sense of purpose and a mutual need for each other's special knowledge.

Derek: I think I can see where this is headed. You're saying any new idea will fail, unless it's adopted by communities of practice.

Vikas: I'm afraid I can't take the credit for that. Actually, it was Edgar Schein who said organizational learning is a three-step process. An idea is articulated by academics, then picked up by members of the consulting community who sell the programme to their corporate clients; and finally the programme is implemented within the firm. But this is where its success or failure depends on its acceptability to the communities of practice.

Almost anybody who has worked in an organization can tell you about so-called 'flavours of the month' which excite a few people, while others feel they are a nuisance that get in the way of doing real work. The problem may not be with the idea itself, but with winning cross-cultural commitment. For example, 'Garibi Hatao' was and is a great idea, but it hasn't been as successful as it might have been because of low commitment on the part of politicians and bureaucrats, the relevant community of practice in this case.

John Seely Brown and Estee Solomon Gray put it nicely by describing organizations as 'webs of participation'. According to them, if you want to change the organization, just change the patterns of participation. There is no way you can compel enthusiasm and commitment from knowledge workers. And without that, you can't create a successful organization. The only way to create a winning company is get workers to choose to opt in, to voluntarily make a commitment to their colleagues.

Derek: So how do you get workers to want to opt in?

Vikas: Alan M Webber put it really well when he said the journey into knowledge management 'begins with technology and leads inexorably to trust'. As for the entire process of managing knowledge, hear out John

Micklethwait and Adrian Wooldridge of *The Economist*. According to them, it involves sucking in ideas, making sure they circulate, encouraging bold experimentation — and that includes not punishing failure — setting up empowered cross-functional teams, and listening closely to the customer.

Derek: Whoa, I'm up to my ears in theory. But can all this actually be implemented in large, complex organizations?

Vikas: Well, they don't get much larger or more complex than General Electric. So, it's worth listening to Jack Welch — who ran the place successfully for twenty years. According to Welch, there's nothing more important than taking everyone's best ideas and transferring them to others. The first step is being open to the best of what everyone, everywhere has to offer. The second is transferring the learning across the organization. In his autobiography, he devotes lots of space to the benefits of Work-Out.

Derek: Work-Out? I know a healthy mind resides in a healthy body, but what's exercising got to do with knowledge management?

Vikas: Work-Out, as it's understood in GE, resulted from Welch's desire to replicate the passion and candour he witnessed during one-to-ones with frontline executives at the company's Crotonville campus throughout the workplace. Let's hear more about it from the man himself:

～

Work-Out was patterned after the traditional New England town meeting. Groups of forty to a hundred employees were invited to share their views on the business and the bureaucracy that got in their way, particularly approvals, reports, meetings, and measurements.

Work-Out meant just what the words implied: taking unnecessary work out of the system. Toward this end, we expected every business to hold hundreds of Work-Outs. This was going to be a massive programme.

A typical Work-Out lasted two to three days. It started with a presentation by the manager who might issue a challenge or outline a broad agenda and then leave. Without the boss present and with a facilitator to grease the discussions, employees were asked to list problems, debate solutions, and be prepared to sell their ideas when the boss returned. The neutral outside facilitator, one of two dozen academics drafted by Jim Baughman, made the exchanges between the employees and the manager go a lot easier.

The real novelty here was that we insisted managers make on-the-spot decisions on each proposal. They were expected to give a yes-or-no decision on at least 75 per cent of the ideas. If a decision couldn't be made on the spot, there was an agreed-upon date for a decision. No one could bury the proposals. As people saw their ideas getting instantly implemented, it became a true bureaucracy buster.

I'll never forget attending one of the Work-Out sessions in April 1990 in our appliance business. Together with thirty employees, we were sitting in a conference room in Lexington, Kentucky, at a Holiday Inn. A union production worker was in the middle of a presentation on how to improve the manufacturing of refrigerator doors. He was describing a part of the process that occurred on the second floor of the assembly line.

Suddenly, the chief steward of the plant jumped up to interrupt him. 'That's BS,' he said. 'You don't know what the hell you're talking about. You've never been up there.'

He grabbed a Magic Marker and began scribbling on the easel in the front of the room. Before you knew it, he had taken over the presentation and had the answer. His solution was accepted immediately.

It was absolutely mind-blowing to see two union guys arguing over a manufacturing process improvement. Imagine kids just out of college with shiny new degrees trying to fix this manufacturing process. They wouldn't have a chance. Here were the guys with experience, helping us fix things.

Small wonder that people began to forget their roles. They started speaking up everywhere.

By mid-1992, more than 200,000 GE employees had been involved in Work-Outs. The rationale for the programme could be summed up by the comment made by a middle-aged appliance worker: 'For twenty-five years,' he said, 'you've paid for my hands when you could have had my brain as well — for nothing.'

Work-Out confirmed what we already knew, that the people closest to the work know it best. Almost every good thing that has happened in the company can be traced to the liberation of some business, some team, or an individual. Work-Out liberated many of them. From a simple idea hatched at Crotonville, Work-Out helped us to create a culture where everyone began playing a part, where everyone's ideas began to count, and where leaders led rather than controlled. They coached — rather than preached — and they got better results.

Derek: So Work-Out was basically about harnessing GE's internal knowledge.

Vikas: Yes, but Welch also recognized that knowledge comes from a variety of unexpected sources. He loathed the N-I-H (Not Invented Here) syndrome. And he proved it by enthusiastically adopting kanban from Japanese companies and the Motorola-pioneered Six Sigma, which involves attaining a quality level where you have fewer than 3.4 defects per million operations.

Incidentally, one of Welch's all-time favourite ideas didn't come from a corporate source. He had told all GE businesses they either had to be number one or number two in their market, or he'd get rid of them. But then, a guy pointed out that GE had plenty of intelligent leaders who could narrowly define their markets to remain safely entrenched in leadership positions. Look at it this way, if I come first or second in one of your quizzes, in which there are only three participants, that's no big deal. But if I won an all-

India quiz with hundreds of participants, then I'd be a real cat.

So GE decided to redefine its markets in such a way that none of its businesses would have a market share of more than 10 per cent. According to Welch, this was both a mind-expanding exercise as well as a market-expanding breakthrough. And guess who was the guy who gave the idea?

Derek: Some management guru?

Vikas: Not quite. It was an army colonel. He was at Crotonville on a four-day visit along with the rest of his batch from the US War College, because one of the GE instructors wanted to throw in these guys with regular corporate executives and see what happened.

Derek: Just goes to show that sometimes, Colonel Knowledge can outrank General Knowledge.

CHAPTER 9

Info-clutter: When More Is Less

Derek: Well, we certainly seem to have come a long long way from the time when knowledge was a jealously guarded commodity. These days, we just seem to be giving it away.

Vikas: True. But frankly, I'm beginning to get a little worried. I just finished re-reading *The Brothers Karamazov*. And I can't get one thought out of my head. Remember Ivan Karamazov saying, 'if everything is permissible, nothing is permissible'? I can't help wondering if that's just as true of information.

Derek: Let me get this straight. After all this talk about how great knowledge is, you're now asking whether we're having too much of a good thing?

Vikas: Not quite. Let's go back to that old difference between information and knowledge. Are we now suffering from information overload? And is that hampering our quest for knowledge?

As you yourself said, information which once used to

be rare and precious has now become plentiful. In fact, I'd say it's becoming so plentiful that it's severely testing the average human's capacity to cope. David Shenk has coined a term to describe this situation: data smog.

Shenk never tires of pointing out that one weekday edition of the *New York Times* contains more information than the average person in seventeenth century England was likely to come across in an entire lifetime. Now, try this on for a little perspective. According to Nicholas Negroponte in *Being Digital,* a fiber the size of a human hair can deliver every issue ever made of the *Wall Street Journal* in less than one second. And you can make as many fibers as you need.

Derek: Hang on a minute. Aren't you taking a Luddite line against technology?

Vikas: Does Steve Jobs sound like a Luddite to you? He's the guy who set up Apple the first time around and gave it a new lease of life with the iMac. Not quite your typical technophobe, is he? Well, Jobs is on record as saying that he's probably spearheaded giving away more computer equipment to schools than anybody else. But he's concluded that more technology does not necessarily equal more knowledge. Lincoln didn't have a website at his log cabin, and he turned

out just fine. After all, as any educator worth her salt would tell you, education is about teaching people how to think, not just overloading them with facts.

Derek: Point taken. But isn't Bill Gates absolutely evangelical about putting information at everyone's fingertips?

Vikas: Yes, he is. But is that necessarily a good thing? Peter Sellers wasn't being funny when he said that when information wasn't so easily acquired, the actual act of finding something had value. But now that it is so easy and plentiful, it simply doesn't have the same value.

In fact, not only is information available in plenty, it's actually flooding us. The typical business manager is said to read a million words per week. Humans are bombarded with more and more advertising and sound bites — whose average length is shrinking all the time. Faxes and e-mails pour in. Pagers, cellphones, laptops — there's virtually no longer any place where one can be free with one's own thoughts. And we happily go along with that.

All this, however, has a price. Every day, our brains reel under the strain of handling a never-ending stream of words, sounds, pictures. Our minds are always churning, working overtime to process the data that keeps pouring in. We are, quite literally, burning out.

There's a looming ADD (Attention Deficit Disorder) epidemic. This increasingly common brain imbalance causes acute restlessness and a propensity toward boredom and distraction. And, of course, more and more of us are living with heightened stress, weakened vision, memory lapses, confusion — all the result of information overstimulation.

Ironically, though, we never quite seem to get over our blind faith in technology. Let me quote some words to you. '(This is) destined to provide greater knowledge to large numbers of people, truer perception of the meaning of current events, more accurate appraisal of men in public life, and a broader understanding of the needs and aspirations of our fellow human beings.' Want to guess who said that?

Derek: Umm, one of the Internet pioneers?

Vikas: Not quite. David Sarnoff, the man who unveiled the first colour television in 1939. From that vision to idiot box, TV sure has come a long way. Children in the US now spend an average of 22,000 hours watching TV before graduating from high school. Psychologists fret about how all this is affecting their reading abilities, their imaginativeness and also their language skills.

There's a sense of paradise lost when one re-reads *Being Digital*. Negroponte mentions getting an e-mail from a high school sophomore called Michael Schrag, who asked if he could visit Negroponte at MIT's renowned Media Lab. Negroponte met both Michael and his father. And Schrag senior couldn't stop gushing about how all sorts of people, including Nobel Prize winners and senior executives, seemed to have all the time in the world to respond to Michael's mails.

Alas, these words, written just a few years back, already sound like they belong to another, hopelessly innocent era. Given the levels of junk and spam mails and viruses floating around cyberspace, Michael's mails would today probably be deleted without even being opened. Computer science expert Michael Dertouzos said a few years ago, 'E-mail is an open duct into your central nervous system. It occupies the brain and reduces productivity'. I think a lot more people are taking him seriously today than when he spoke those words.

Derek: OK, so we're paying a price. But don't people know a lot more today than they did earlier?

Vikas: Do they? Worries about 'dumbing down' are a worldwide phenomenon. We've seen stories in leading Indian magazines about Generation Y's complete lack of general knowledge. In the US, a survey some years ago showed that two-fifths of all American college students thought prehistoric people had to protect themselves from dinosaurs, thoroughly unaware that there was a 65-million-year span between the last dinosaur and the first human. I'm not sure Indians would do much better today, especially after watching *Jurassic Park*.

Political scientist Eric Smith concluded from dismal knowledge surveys that in the US, there had been virtually no improvement in general knowledge over a period of forty years. Beyond a point, people seem to either forget things or simply tune out. Guess we shouldn't have been so hard on George W Bush when he flunked an impromptu general knowledge test while contesting for the US presidency.

Derek: Maybe, but for every George W Bush, there's also a Bill Clinton. And I don't think even his worst critics denied that Clinton was an intelligent, well-informed person?

Vikas: Sure he was. Which is why he was probably the first US president ever to be dubbed a dataholic. Indeed, White House staffers during Clinton's term actually complained to journalist Elizabeth Drew about 'paralysis by analysis'. According to them, meetings never accomplished anything because Clinton never stopped thinking. I guess you could say that while Bush has dodged information overload, Clinton soaked it all in.

Derek: There's just no satisfying some people, is there?

Vikas: Note, please, that while Clinton could probably write volumes on morality, that didn't necessarily make him a more moral person.

Which brings up another concern: what Shenk terms the 'coarsening of culture'. In order to cut through the communication clutter, communicators are constantly upping the ante. Confronted with an audience that has metaphorically plugged its ears, covered its eyes and wrapped itself in a protective coccoon, they respond by shrieking at the top of their voice, using bright, glaring lights, and thumping people's heads to get their attention.

Films are becoming more and more sexually explicit and violent. Every new action movie plumbs new depths of gruesome realism, while advertising is becoming increasingly tasteless. Music divas compete to show the most skin in their videos, and rappers who extol murdering policemen and having incestuous relationships become chart-toppers. Subjects that were once the preserve of seedy niche publications are increasingly staple fare for respected mass media outfits. Political commentators never tire of talking about the declining level of political discourse in the US — and I think most people would agree that's a worldwide phenomenon.

Derek: But this coarsening is happening because people are tuning out. Which means that some form of self-preservation is kicking in, right? Besides, people do find short-cuts through info clutter, don't they?

Vikas: Well, Negroponte has observed that the value of information about information can sometimes be greater than the value of the information itself. That would certainly explain the popularity of Google, which claims to have indexed over 2 billion Web pages. In a situation where people have more information than they know what to do with, anybody who can filter and prioritize information is going to be extremely welcome.

Unfortunately, excessive filtering can have its pitfalls. Which is why many of us seem to know more and more about less and less, with eclecticism being sacrificed at the altar of specialization. Decades ago, Friedrich Nietzsche foresaw this. Remember that passage in *Thus Spake Zarathustra*, in which the prophet asks a scientist whether he is a specialist in the ways of the leech. The scientist responds: 'That would be something immense; how could I presume to do so! That, however, of which I am master and knower, is the brain of the leech; that is my world! For the sake of this did I cast everything else aside, for the sake of this did everything else become indifferent to me.'

Literary exaggeration? Maybe. But how many of us haven't encountered at least one academically brilliant person who is woefully unaware about anything not contained in textbooks? How many urban dwellers can truthfully say they don't feel some identification with Earl Shorris, who posits that the so-called global village has actually become a bunch of electronic cottages populated by isolated dreamers? In our quest for specialized knowledge, we are all — to some degree or other — becoming social misfits.

Derek: So what do you want to do? Roll back time?

Vikas: No, I realize that's impossible. But as we careen our way through communication clutter, here's a thought I'd like to leave you with. There was an ad that went, 'It's a small world. All addresses start with "www".' True. But knowledge, perhaps, is about discovering the large world that we carry around within us. As we immerse ourselves ever more in the small world, are we increasingly losing touch with the bigger one?

CHAPTER 10

Who's Smart? Who's Not? Who Knows?

Derek: Specialist, generalist... we've seen that the quest for knowledge is a search in many directions.

Bunny Suraiya: Yes, right. To do a quick recap, there is the search for the definition of knowledge: What is it? Perceptions or ideas? Essence or existence?

There is the search for methods of acquiring knowledge: How do we gain it? By learning facts? By thinking laterally? By Zen techniques?

Then there is the search for measuring knowledge: How do we know how much we know? In short, what is our Knowledge Quotient?

Derek: Right! Now, we've come down to the crunch. Let's talk about KQ.

Bunny: In a sense, in every test or examination at school, college and university, the resulting grades could be considered a sort of KQ — but limited to only a given number of subjects. To assess the individual as an entity with areas of knowledge encompassing social, professional, recreational and self-knowledge — in addition to syllabus or book learning — we need to go further in the methodology of testing.

Let's take a quick look at some of the methods of knowledge testing that have been used over the years.

Plato's method of testing knowledge was very simple: He merely looked at your social rank. The higher up it was, the more intelligent you were. He believed that God or nature endowed certain individuals with more intelligence than others. As a result, those individuals rose to become the social elite, who then propagated themselves so that biology determined intelligence and intelligence determined biology in an endless circle.

Derek: Huh! What about today's brilliant entrepreneurs — most of them self-made!

Bunny: You're right, Derek. It doesn't take much to see the limitations of the Platonic method of gauging knowledge. One need only look at the arrant stupidity of the aristocrats whose misgovernance led to the French and Russian Revolutions.

Nonetheless, in the late nineteenth century, Sir Francis Galton, a cousin of Charles Darwin, decided that Plato's beliefs were basically sound and that intelligence was a biological inheritance. His dream was to 'breed' a superior society and to do so, he required to be able to measure intelligence in a scientific manner.

But the questionnaires he devised to test natural ability assumed that, being biologically given, intelligence must be visible in all individual activities, from the simplest motor activities to complex thought patterns. Thus, he reckoned that we could get a fair estimation of an individual's mental powers by measuring his physical ones.

Derek: Attempting to gauge the invisible by the visible?

Bunny: Exactly! Today we know much more than to assume that if X cannot ride a bicycle then he also cannot understand arithmetic. But even so, the modern IQ test owes much to Galton's view of intelligence as biologically determined and his attempt to devise an instrument to measure it.

At the turn of the nineteenth century, Alfred Binet (1857-1911), working at the Sorbonne in Paris, first decided to measure intelligence by using a method developed by his compatriot, Paul Broca: measuring the cranium. The assumption was that a bigger cranium could accommodate a bigger brain; a bigger brain could 'hold' more intelligence.

However, after years spent measuring school children's heads and conducting five full-scale studies, Binet found that the average difference between good and poor student's head measurements amounted to a mere millimeter! Though disappointed, he was honest enough to question even this millimetric difference in size, confessing his fear that it was his own bias towards poorer students that had made him perceive it.

Persevering, he turned to another approach. Constructing a scale of hodge-podge activities which combined tests of general knowledge, memory, attention, imagination, comprehension, aesthetic judgements (which face is prettier?), moral/ethical judgements, counting and so on, Binet assigned an age level to each task , calling it the 'mental' age. To arrive at their own mental ages, children began the Binet tests with tasks for the youngest age and progressed in sequence until they could no longer complete the tasks. The age associated with the last tasks they could perform became their 'mental age'. Intelligence was calculated by subtracting this mental age from the chronological age.

But in 1912, the German psychologist William Stern proposed that dividing the mental age by the chronological age was more accurate than subtracting it because, for example, a two-year disparity between mental age two and chronological age four displays a far greater degree of mental impairment than a similar two-year disparity between mental age sixteen and chronological age eighteen. By Binet's method, however, the levels of mental impairment in both cases would be seen as the same, a clear inaccuracy. Stern's proposal was accepted as a breakthrough and the IQ equation as we know it was born.

IQ = mental age x 100 (this step is to eliminate the decimal point) / Chronological age

Derek: But now we know that IQ tests are far from foolproof.

Bunny: Yes we do. And to be fair to Binet, many of the drawbacks of IQ ranking were foreseen by him, and much of its misuse might have been averted had Binet's often-expressed fears been heeded. He saw his tests chiefly as a tool to identify weak students with a view to coaching them to reach their optimal levels of performance. He refused to label IQ as inborn intelligence, and he was afraid that schoolteachers might do so, thereby giving up on weaker students who were the very ones needing their teachers' greatest efforts.

Binet declined too, to regard his IQ scale as a

device for ranking everyone's mental ability. He devised it solely for the limited purpose of identifying children whose poor performance indicated a need for special tuition. In fact, the IQ scale presented a norm. For anyone to be below the norm was a matter for concern; to score above the basic figure was irrelevant. How far we have come from Binet, when people boast of their high IQs as God-given privileges!

Derek: And worse, in recent years, IQ testing has been sharply criticized for being biased in favour of racial and cultural majorities, which results in people of minority races and cultures habitually seeming to have a low IQ.

Bunny: Exactly. To illustrate this point, let's go back for a moment to our Kalahari bushman and our New York executive. An IQ test devised by the elders of the bush tribe would be impossible for the New Yorker to pass, it is doubtful if he would even understand the questions. The bushman would find an American IQ test a similar, incomprehensible nightmare.

And that's not all. There's another problem with conventional testing, which is quite simply this: who guarantees the ability of the tester to know more than the person being tested?

Derek : I must say I sometimes thought some of my

teachers at school didn't know enough. Is that what you mean?

Bunny: Something like that. In *The Society of Mind*, Marvin Minsky gives us a Jack-and-Mary example. Suppose Jack is the tester or examiner and he tells us that 'Mary knows geometry'. What does that really mean to you or me? For all we know, Mary might believe that circles are square, and it happens that Jack agrees! Jack's statement tells us more about Jack than about Mary!

So what can we do? If we can't even measure intelligence, how can we measure knowledge, which is the cornerstone of intelligence? Just when it's beginning to look like an impossibility, there's light at the end of the tunnel. Derek, you should take over here.

Derek: Right! My new methodology focuses on KQ instead of on the discredited IQ. The next chapter introduces the only multidimensional, multi-functional and universal method of knowing how much you know. A method by which you can test yourself and match your score against the knowledge bank of the world. On any subject. Any time. And get an accurate measurement of your Knowledge Quotient at the time, depending on how many people around the world have

more or less knowledge of your chosen subject than you do.

Bunny: The unique thing about KQ is that you can improve your scores by learning more about your subject. And learning more about your subject is what you do each time you test yourself.

That's the true beauty of KQ testing. Perhaps we could rephrase the old saying to read that it is possible to test your KQ and raise it too!

CHAPTER II

The Seamless Robe of KQ

Bunny: There's a short story I read years ago, which is a sort of parable to illustrate the breadth of KQ. Let me share it with you.

This is an O Henry story about a notable New York dandy, famous for the fastidious attention he paid to his clothes, who caused great consternation among his many admirers in high society by suddenly disappearing from their ken. Finally, a rumour was heard that a person answering to the missing person's description had taken up residence as an inmate in a remote Greek monastery run by an order of monks known for their extreme austerity. Intrigued, several of the absconding socialite's friends decided to investigate and journeyed to the distant monastery. There, the visitors were shown into a cell bare of all furniture except for some low wooden stools. After a while, a monk wearing the simple coarse robe of the order walked in. The man's face wore an expression of beatific contentment, and it took the New Yorkers a moment to realize that this was indeed their lost friend, but utterly transformed as though a light had been turned on within.

The New Yorkers urged their erstwhile companion to come back to the glittering salons of Manhattan. But the man in the robe merely smiled and shook his head. He said had found perfect peace and happiness in the monastery and never wished to return to the world he had left behind. 'But how can you leave the glamour and the luxury you enjoyed there for this dismal, uncomfortable place?' his friends persisted.

The monk smiled again and replied, 'All my life, I had one great obsession: How and where could I find a garment in which, when I sat down, the cloth covering my knees wouldn't wrinkle. The best tailors of New York, London and Paris couldn't solve my problem. Then I heard about this place and came here. And see — when I sit, my robe doesn't wrinkle at all across my knees.'

Master storyteller that he was, O Henry leaves it for readers to reach their own conclusions. Had the dandy, true to his essential nature, found spiritual happiness in his own dandy fashion? Or did he merely use the unwrinkleable robe as a metaphor to explain to his former associates a concept of bliss which otherwise would be inexplicable to those steeped in worldly knowledge?

Either way, the story is clear about one point:

perfection can be attained by many paths of knowledge; spiritual or sartorial, it makes no difference.

Derek: I see where you're going with this and where the KQ connection comes in. Go on...

Bunny: O Henry's fable is a precursor to the philosophy of KQ. Unlike other indicators of mental competence — like IQ, for instance — which were seriously flawed in that they were based on a one-sided or unidimensional view of the mind and its activity, KQ is multidimensional and multifunctional. It recognizes many, equally valid knowledge skills. From the water-finding abilities of the Kalahari bushman, to the portfolio management of the Wall Street analyst. What you know, or what you choose to know and excel in, is dependent on your environment and your choice of career and lifestyle within that environment.

Derek: That's right. The true beauty of KQ lies in the fact that it does not assume any given level of knowledge in the user. And the method does not change from subject to subject. This is why KQ testing is as free from bias as it is possible to be in an imperfect world.

Bunny: KQ is equally relevant to all: a dandy in New

York, a monk in a cell, a survivor in the wilderness, an ambitious corporate executive. For KQ is the personalized key which opens the safe deposit vault of self-attainment that is within each of us. All we have to do is find and fashion the key most suitable for each of us.

There are many keys to select from: Career KQ, Leisure KQ, Social KQ, Educational KQ, Self KQ...

Bunny: That sounds great, Derek. But how exactly does KQ work?

Derek: See, it's like this. KQ tests feature verbal, written and visual facts to measure individual knowledge in any subject. This is unique to KQ, as is the format of the tests. A typical set of ten questions on any subject will include testing of decision-making skills, testing of depth as well as breadth of knowledge, testing of analytical skills and logical skills. Every set of ten questions in any random sequence will always contain all of these tests in written, audio or video form.

Bunny: So how is a person's KQ calculated?

Derek: It's quite an ingenious method though I do say it myself! KQ is the ratio between the actual difficulty and the perceived difficulty in answering any set of ten questions in any particular field of knowledge.

What we do is give each question a Perceived Difficulty Number. Now when a person answers the question, depending on how long they take to answer — and how correctly they answer, we get what we call an Actual Difficulty reading. The smaller the gap between the Perceived Difficulty and the Actual Difficulty experienced by the person, the higher the KQ. It's quite simple, really.

Bunny: Yes, it certainly sounds simple. The only thing is, how do you attach a Perceived Difficulty Number to any question. Is it arbitrary or what?

Derek: No, not arbitrary at all; that wouldn't be fair! Discovering the perceived Difficulty Number of any question is a two-level exercise.

First, we throw open the questions to the whole population — if I can call it that — of the World Wide Web.

The first person to answer a question or questions correctly will form the reference point for the second person and so on. In this way, we will use all the questions to get the Perceived Difficulty Number for each question. Over a period of time, as more and more users take the tests, these numbers will become more and more accurate.

Bunny: You mentioned two ways?

Derek: Yes. The second way is this: We administer the test offline, under supervision, to an unbiased sample to get more numbers and then get a fixed number for each question. This will eliminate the in-built bias of online Perceived Difficulty Numbers where there is no supervision.

Bunny: So what you're saying is basically that an individual's KQ is relative to other people's. So then surely it can vary over time...

Derek: Yes. It can go up or down. The model we use also takes into account the possibility that a number of people might take part in the exercise; their backgrounds (during offline tests) and so on. The model can also give you your KQ changes within a given range of perceived difficulty. It can also tell you what percentage of people are above or below you for a given KQ score.

When an individual takes the test we are able to track their recall time, the number of question they got right, how much information (or meaning) they can extract per unit time to get to the right answer. And then we compare the individual score with others who have taken the test.

Bunny: And voila! You can give that individual his or her KQ Score!

You're right, it is rather ingenious. I'm ready to find out my own KQ score. And I'm sure Jug and Vikas will want to check theirs too.

This is good stuff, Derek. It means that whether you're a bushman, a corporate honcho or a student, the KQ system can really help everyone to compare themselves with the rest of the world and measure how much — or how little — they are in the know of things. Am I right?

Derek: Spot on. You got it!

Index

Accenture, 76
Actual Difficulty, 111
America, 62
Anderson, Philip, 72
Apple, 88
Aristotle, 2, 6, 8
Attention Deficit Disorder
  (ADD), 90

Bach, J. S., 16
Baughman, Jim, 83
Being Digital, 88, 91
Bell, A.J., 59
Berkeley, George, 23, 25
Binet, Alfred, 99, 100-01
Blair, Tony, 17
Bodhidharma, 40
Bowman, Dave, 14
Britain, 17
British,
  empiricist philosophy, 23
  spy, 33
Broca, Paul, 99
Brothers Karamazov, The,
  87
Brown, John Seely, 81
Buddhist monastery, 48
Burali-Forti, 56

Bush, George W., 93
Byrne, John A., 84

Cambridge, 57
Cartesian system, 20
China, 30, 38, 40
Chola, 16
Clarke, Arthur C., 48
Clinton, Bill, 93, 94
Columbus, Christopher, 62
Communism, 33
Communities of practice,
  79-81
Copernicus, 36
Corporate Dossier, 76
Cruise, Tom, 17

*Dancing Wu-li Masters,
  The*, 37
Darwin, Charles, 32, 98
Data smog, 88
de Lamarck, Jean Baptiste
  Pierre Antoine de Monet,
  32
Deming, W Edward, 64
Dertouzos, Michael, 92
Descartes, Rene, 20-21
Dow Jones Index, 16

Drew, Elizabeth, 93
Drucker, Peter, 61-65, 67
Dualism, 23

Eco, Umberto, 29
Economic Times, 73
Economist, 81
Einstein, 36
Epimenides paradox, 54-56
Epistemology, 2, 31
Escher's Print Gallery, 54
Europe, 51, 61-62
Eve, 28

Factoid, 30-34
Finkelstein, Sydney, 72
Ford, Henry, 63
Freedom of choice, 12
French Revolution, 98

Galileo, 36
Galton, Sir Francis, 98-99
Garden of Eden, 28
Gates, Bill, 90
General Electric, 82, 84-86
Generation Y, 92
Germany, 62
Godel, Kurt, 54-55
  Incompleteness Theorem, 54-55
Google, 95
Gordian knot, 54
Gray, Estee Solomon, 81
Gulag, 33
Gutenberg, 61

Heisenberg, Werner, 25, 41, 43, 45, 53
  Principle of Indeterminacy, 41, 53
Himalayas, 48
Hofstadt, Douglas R, 54
Holmes, Sherlock, 13-14, 16, 36
Holocaust, 31
Hope, Jeremy, 71, 73, 76-77, 80
Hope, Tony, 71, 73, 76-77, 80
Hume, David, 23-24

India, 9, 40, 76
Indian philosophy, 28
Infosys, 76
Italy, 30

Jack, Straight from the Gut, 84
Japan, 40
Jobs, Steve, 88
Jurassic Park, 93

Kalahari desert, 10
  bushman, 16, 49-50, 102, 108
'Kaizen', 64
Kant, Emmanuel, 45-47
  Critique of Pure Reason, 45
Kidman, Nicole, 17
Knowledge management, 70-71

Knowledge Quotient, 97
Knowledge workers, 61,
    63, 65-67, 70, 81
Koan, 41
Kochikar, V. P., 76

Lenat, Douglas B, 14
Leonard-Barton, Dorothy,
    76
Liebniz, Gottfried Wilhelm,
    51, 53
Lincoln, Abraham, 88
Locke, John, 23-24
Luther, Martin, 62
Lysenko, Trofim, 32-33

MIT, Center for
    Organizational Learning,
    79
    Media Lab, 92
Mailer, Norman, 30-31
Manhattan, 10, 50, 107
Manohar, Hemant, 73
Marco Polo, 29-30
Maruti Suzuki, 40
Marx, Groucho, 37-38
Marx, Karl, 63
Marxism, 65
McKinsey, 78
Micklethwait, John, 81
Minsky, Marvin, 103
Monads, 53
Motorola, 85
Mount Everest, 9

Negroponte, Nicholas, 88,

91-92, 95
Nehru, Jawaharlal, 9
New York, 10, 110
    executive, 15, 102
    subway, 16
New York Times, 88
Newton, Isaac, 36
Nietzsche, Friedrich, 95
Nobel Prize, 25, 92

O Henry, 106-08
Orwell, George, 31-32

Perceived Difficulty
    Number, 111-12
Plato, 2, 6, 8, 98
    Platonic, 23
pro-Nazi historians, 31
Principia Mathematica, 56-
    57
Protestant Reformation, 62
Ptolemy, 36
Pythagoras's theorem, 16

Quinn, James Brian, 72

Reich, Robert, 63
    'symbolic analysts', 63
Russel, Bertrand, 56
Russian Revolution, 98

Sanskrit, 40
Sarnoff, David, 91
Schein, Edgar, 79, 80
Schrodinger, Erwin, 27, 28
Sellers, Peter, 90

Shankara, 28
Shenk, David, 88, 94
  'coarsening of culture',
  94, 95
Shorris, Earl, 96
Six Sigma, 85
Smith, Eric, 93
Society of Mind, The, 103
Socrates, 2, 6, 8
Sorbonne, 99
Stalin, 33
Stalinism, 32
Steel, Chaparral, 76
Stern, William, 100-01

Taylor, Frederick Winslow,
  63-65
  labour productivity, 64
Theory of relativity, 36
Third Wave, The, 67
Thirty-Year War, 51
Thus Spake Zarathustra, 95
Toffler, Alvin, 67

Total Quality Management
  (TQM), 64
Tree of Knowledge, 28

USA, 9, 31, 92, 93, 95

Vietnam war, 30-31

Wall Street Journal, 16, 88
Wall Street tycoon, 49-50,
  108
Washington DC, 9
Watson, 13
Webber, Alan M., 78, 81
Welch, Jack, 82, 84-85
White House, 93
Whitehead, A.N., 56
Wooldridge, Adrian, 81
Work-Out, 82-85

Zen, 40-41, 43, 97
  Buddhist, 43
Zulov, Gary, 37